D0955937

How Not to be the Perfect

Boss

This is a STAR FIRE book

STAR FIRE BOOKS
Crabtree Hall, Crabtree Lane
Fulham, London SW6 6TY
United Kingdom

www.star-fire.co.uk

First published 2008

08 10 12 11 09

1 3 5 7 9 10 8 6 4 2

Star Fire is part of The Foundry Creative Media Company Limited

ISBN: 978 1 84786 203 7

Printed in China

Thanks to: Chelsea Edwards and Nick Wells

Picture Credits
Images courtesy of Shutterstock: page 7, 11 © Susan Kehoe; 8 © Oksana Perkins; 13, 15
© James Pierce; 17 © Victor Burnside; 19 © Nancy Hixson; 20 © Ruben Olavo Vicente;
23 © Alexey Zarubin; 27 © Steffen Foerster Photography; 28 © Gail Johnson; 31 ©
Meredith Lamb; 34 © Pascal Janssen; 39 © Jonathan Pais; 45 © Larsek; 47, 72 © Hans
Meerbeek; 48 © Andrey Kozachenko; 51 © Roman Kobzarev; 52 © Tomo Jesenicnik;
4, 55 © Natthawat Wongrat; 56, © Larsek; 4, 59 © UltraOrto, S.A.; 60 © Jeff Gynane;
63 © Brandon Mayoral; 65 © N Joy Neish; 66 © Johan Swanepoel; 71 © Michael Rubin

Images courtesy of iStockphoto: page 24 © Stephanie DeLay; 32 © Pauline Mills; 36 ©
Vladimir Mucibabic; 41 © John Pitcher; 4, 42 © Jeroen Peys; 1, 3, 69 © Heiko Grossman

How Not to be the Perfect

Boss

Ulysses Brave

STAR FIRE

Foreword

Being a boss is hard. Everyone expects
you to know what to do, but of course you
rarely do. Many tell me that their employees
have unreasonable expectations of their
employers, so after much brainstorming,
and thinking out of the box, I have decided
to offer some careful advice based on
simple common sense.

Ulysses Brave

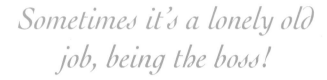

Sometimes it's a lonely old job, being the boss!

Outward Bound management courses can sometimes lead to a passionate office romance.

There are times, at the end of another heavy day at the top, when it's just too hard to take that long journey home.

It can be a challenge to exchange sensitive personnel information in an open plan office.

Rivalry between
directors can get a little
out of hand.

After a day of terrorizing the employees, the boss comes home and is swiftly put in his place.

A good few glasses of wine at lunchtime will always go down well with a boss of a certain generation.

It is always awkward when the boss has to mention an employee's body odour problem.

There is always one last resort when the profits are hit by poor trading, and shareholder confidence is low.

Occasionally try to eat in the canteen with your employees.

*Even bosses have
bad hair days.*

Retirement is close...

Another day worrying
about the cash flow.

Sometimes board meetings just go on too long...

Some bosses are just too handsome to be let out on their own — or so <u>they</u> think.

*Always appoint
your friends to investigate
the fairness of executive pay.*

If someone from accounts questions your expenses, just remind them who is boss.

Have you felt recently that technology is moving too quickly for you?

Make sure that major shareholders are invited to enjoy the benefits of your success.

Catching flies while frightening the staff can provide a pleasing diversion from the stress of the day.

Good manners are at the heart of all good managers.

Big bosses like to train up little bosses to take over the company one day.

Don't be tempted to have an affair with the good-looking new marketing officer.

An afternoon nap is a tax-efficient perk for the quick-minded boss.

Make sure you find a luxurious executive chair, one worthy of your exalted status.

Try to be more convincing with your smile at the staff meeting.

It's not just employees who yearn for another hour in bed in the mornings...

Happy is the day when all customers pay on time.

After many years at the top,
some bosses let themselves
go, thinking that no-one
will notice. They do.

A good old-fashioned boss
will always put their
blinkers on first thing
in the morning.

Improve your own success by encouraging competition in middle management.

Another hard day sorting out
the sales department.

Try to maintain
your dignity when
giving instructions.

Come back soon!